I0811413

To

From

Written and compiled by Deborah Lock
Illustrations copyright © 2015, 2017, 2018, 2019 Antonia Woodward
This edition copyright © 2021 Lion Hudson IP Limited

The right of Antonia Woodward to be identified as the illustrator of this work has been asserted by her in accordance with the Copyright, Designs and Patents Act 1988.

All rights reserved. No part of this publication may be reproduced or transmitted in any form or by any means, electronic or mechanical, including photocopy, recording, or any information storage and retrieval system, without permission in writing from the publisher.

Published by
Lion Hudson Limited
Wilkinson House, Jordan Hill Business Park
Banbury Road, Oxford OX2 8DR, England
www.lionhudson.com

ISBN 978 0 7459 7922 9

First edition 2021

Acknowledgments
All prayers by Deborah Lock, Sophie Piper, and Elena Pasquali are copyright © Lion Hudson IP Limited

A catalogue record for this book is available from the British Library

Printed and bound in China, March 2021, LH54

Bedtime Prayers

Illustrated by Antonia Woodward

LION CHILDREN'S

It is the end of the day
and time to pray,
So I close my eyes
and think about my day.
I will praise God
and thank God.
I will ask God
and listen to God.
I am ready
to spend time with God.

Contents

Praise for the World

All things bright and beautiful,
All creatures great and small.
All things wise and wonderful,
The Lord God made them all.

Cecil Frances Alexander

Thank you for the world around me.
The birds that fly,
The fish that swim,
The animals that run.

The flowers that open,
The trees that grow,
The fruit that ripen.
The sun that shines,
The wind that blows,
The rain that pours.
Thank you for the world around me.

Thanks for My Day

Thank you for being with me today:
My fun times,
My sad times,
My busy times,
My quiet times.
What a day!

Bless the window
Bless the door
Bless the ceiling
Bless the floor
Bless this place which is our home
Bless us as we go and come.

Sophie Piper

Bless the food I taste
to keep strong and healthy.
Bless the things I touch
as I work and play.

Bless the sights I see
as I look around me.
Bless the things I smell
as I go from place to place.
Bless the sounds I hear
that fill me with joy.

Sorry for any hurtful words
  I have said,
Sorry for any hurtful actions
  I have done.
You wipe away these words
  and deeds this day,
so tomorrow can be a fresh new one.

At the end of the day
Troubles must be put away
Quarrels must be laid to rest
So that we at peace may rest.

Elena Pasquali

God in heaven, hear my prayer,
Keep me in thy loving care.
Be my guide in all I do,
Bless all those who love me too.

Traditional

Let my life shine
like a star in the night,
filling my world
with goodness and light.
For blessings here
and those in store
we give thanks now
and evermore.

Elena Pasquali

The day is done.
I have put away my toys
and turned off the tech.
I have cleaned my teeth
and brushed my hair.
I have changed my clothes
and washed my face and hands.
I have read my book
and hugged my family.
I am tucked up in bed
and ready to close my eyes.
My prayers are said.
Goodnight.

Thinking of Others

For my family,
  Thank you, Lord.
For my friends,
  Thank you, Lord.
For my teachers,
  Thank you, Lord.
For my carers,
  Thank you, Lord.
For my ....,
  Thank you, Lord.

Help me to care,
Help me to share,
Help me to be kind.
Help me to be friendly.
Thank you for helping me today.

Remember those who are ill.
Remember those who are lonely.
Remember those who are hungry.
Remember those who are afraid.
Look after them through the day
and through the night.

Dear God, bless all my family,
as I tell you each name;
and please bless each one differently
for no one's quite the same.

Elena Pasquali

God bless all those that I love;
God bless all those that love me;
God bless all those that love those
that I love,
And all those that love those that love me.

From an old New England sampler

Blessings for the Night

I see the moon
And the moon sees me;
God bless the moon
And God bless me.

Traditional

The darkness comes:
Give thanks for the night.
The stars appear:
Give thanks for their light.
The air is still:
Give thanks for the calm.
And God is here:
Keep us safe from harm.

Sophie Piper

baaaa

You made the light.
You are in the dark.
Let me have no fear,
For I know you are here.

The storm may roar,
the wind may blow,
but Love will never
let me go.
The wind may blow,
the storm may roar.
Love keeps me safe
for evermore.

Sophie Piper

Keep safe this night
 everything and everyone.
Bless this night
 everything and everyone.

The moon shines bright,
The stars give light
Before the break of day;
God bless you all
Both great and small
And send a joyful day.

Traditional

Index of first lines